CW01662829

Jesus ABC

Published in 2016 by Very Christ Publishing
www.verychrist.com

ISBN: 978-0-9954764-0-0

Dedication

It is my joy to dedicate this little book to all Christian parents who love and fear God, and accordingly take very seriously God's command to teach His Word diligently to our children. Your obedient labour of love shall not be in vain.

"Train up a child in the way he should go, and when he is old he will not depart from it."

Proverbs 22:6

Acknowledgements

Thank You, Father, for Your prodigious love. You are my joy, my strength, my life and my portion forever. Thank You for the "unspeakable gift" of Jesus Christ our Lord, through Whose merit alone I have become Your child. Thank You for the blessed Holy Spirit leading, teaching, enlightening and comforting me. Thank You for Your holy Word, my true light and my guide.

Thank you also to all true disciples of our Lord Jesus, who have inspired and continue to inspire me spiritually. I thank God for my wonderful family, for all their love and support and prayers.

Specifically, I thank Pastor Caitano de Souza for his encouragement and counsel. Thank you to my son, Tristram, for facilitating the production of this book with his brilliant IT skills. Thank you to my son, Julian, for his judicious editing. Finally, thank you to my husband, Steven, for his love, unceasing support and encouragement.

Contents

Preface

A plea to fellow Christian parents:

Focus not on a "head start",
Give instead a true start.
Wisdom commands a Godstart,
Their eternal gain, a pure heart.

By a "Godstart", we mean the early and thorough grounding of the education of our children in the Word of God. From the very beginning of their learning, our little ones' dark hearts must be exposed to the pure light of God's Word. Our priority must surely be to raise our children as our holy and infinitely wise God commands.

God's Word is clear. Scriptures such as Deuteronomy 6:4-9, Psalm 78:2-8 and Ephesians 6:4 lay out our biblical mandate for teaching our children the ways of God. Obedience to the commands in these verses is crucial. Teach them early, teach them well. Strive to be diligent.

Take all opportunities, use all good means, to let them know and understand who God is. Pray unceasingly that they have a vision of the holiness of God, that they may have an understanding of the true horror of sin, and that this would lead them to repent and trust in Jesus. Have we any greater joy than to see our beloved children walking in the truth? The times that we live in are exceedingly evil and spiritual darkness abounds. We must, by God's grace, prayerfully guard against sinful worldly influences on our children through schools, secular teachers, peers, internet, books, music, computer games and other sources.

Let us whole-heartedly honour God; let us give the greatest gift to our children, give Christ: give a Godstart. May the Lord God bless all your labour in your closest vineyard as you seek to raise, for His glory, Godly children in a wicked and perverse generation.

This little volume is intended as a parent-child devotional for parents seeking to raise their children from a young age in the faith. It explores the character and the work of our Lord Jesus Christ, through small expositions of many of the wonderful names and titles of Jesus as revealed in the Bible. I pray that you and your children will find this book fruitful and enjoyable, as you read it with them. Included are notes to help with doctrine and "big" theological words or phrases like "Lamb of God", "Foundation" and "Redeemer". As you survey the names and titles of Jesus listed here, be sure to engage your children in giving glory to God for each name and what it reveals about Jesus. Teach your children to praise God continually (Psalm 34:1, Psalm 78:4). Let them know that He is worthy of all adoration! May you and your children increase in your personal knowledge of, and your love and service to, our matchlessly beautiful Lord and Saviour, Jesus Christ!

Scripture References

Ephesians 6:4

And you, fathers, do not provoke your children to wrath, but bring them up in the training and admonition of the Lord.

Mark 10:14

Let the little children come to Me, and do not forbid them; for of such is the kingdom of God.

Proverbs 22:6

Train up a child in the way he should go,

And when he is old he will not depart from it.

Deuteronomy 6:4–9

Hear, O Israel: The LORD our God, the Lord *is* one! You shall love the LORD your God with all your heart, with all your soul, and with all your strength.

And these words which I command you today shall be in your heart. You shall teach them diligently to your children, and shall talk of them when you sit in your house, when you walk by the way, when you lie down, and when you rise up. You shall bind them as a sign on your hand, and they shall be as frontlets between your eyes. You shall write them on the doorposts of your house and on your gates.

Psalm 78:2-8

I will open my mouth in a parable;
I will utter dark sayings of old,
Which we have heard and known,
And our fathers have told us.
We will not hide *them* from their children,
Telling to the generation to come the praises of the LORD,
And His strength and His wonderful works that He has done.

For He established a testimony in Jacob,
And appointed a law in Israel,
Which He commanded our fathers,
That they should make them known to their children;
That the generation to come might know *them,*
The children *who* would be born,
That they may arise and declare *them* to their children,
That they may set their hope in God,
And not forget the works of God,
But keep His commandments;
And may not be like their fathers,
A stubborn and rebellious generation,
A generation *that* did not set its heart aright,
And whose spirit was not faithful to God.

Mark 16:15

And He said to them, "Go into all the world and preach the gospel to every creature".

Note to Children

Beloved Child,

Do you know that in Bible times, names often had a special meaning? Isaac, for example, means "laughter", Judah means "praise", and Samuel means "asked of God". Perhaps your name has a meaning.

What about Jesus – the most important and the most magnificent Person ever? What does His name mean?

The Bible tells us that our glorious Lord is called "Jesus" (which means "the Lord saves") because He came to save His people from their sins (Matthew 1:21). The meaning of His name shows His great and amazing mission – a mission beyond compare.

Our Lord Jesus has many other names and titles recorded in the Bible. Each tells us something special about Him. Let us now look at some of these wonderful names as we go through the alphabet. May you praise God with all your heart for every one of His names, because Jesus is truly AWESOME!

Beloved, there is none like Jesus, our Saviour!

May the Lord open your spiritual (inner) eyes, that you may see how glorious and wonderful Jesus is! May you hear His call even now and follow Him with all your heart. May you love Jesus passionately and know that in Him you will find no truer Friend. God bless you mightily.

In Christ, my exceeding joy,

Patricia Newman

A Ω

A is for Alpha

Jesus is the Alpha and Omega;
Jesus, the Start and the End.
How mighty His love is, which makes me so eager
To know Him and serve Him, my Friend.

Jesus says, "I am the Alpha and the Omega, *the* Beginning and *the* End, the First and the Last."
Revelation 22:13

From A to Z, Jesus is the Word of God, declaring and showing what God is like.

Note: *Alpha* is the first letter of the Greek alphabet. *Omega* is the last letter of the Greek alphabet. This wonderful all-encompassing title means that Jesus is everything – He is our all in all. Our greatest need is to know Him and to walk with Him. Jesus is the One through Whom we become children of God (Acts 4:12).

Question: Have you begun your journey with Jesus?

Prayer: Dear Father in heaven, please draw me near to You through the wonderful love of Jesus.

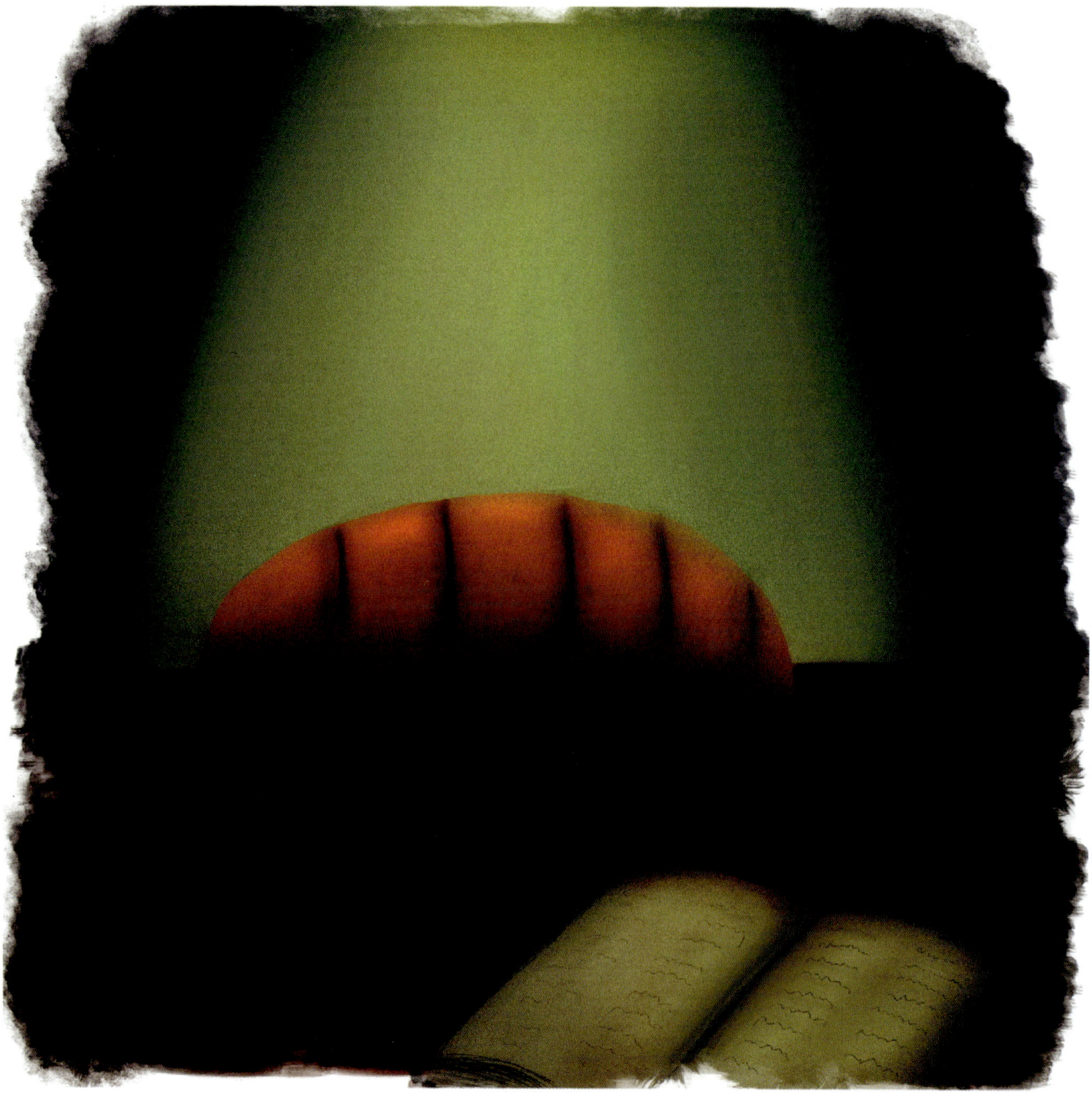

B is for Bread

All children eat bread to live and to grow.
Dear children, be sure to feed on True Bread;
For Jesus came down from above to bestow
The fullness of life by His Spirit and Word.

Jesus says, "I am the bread of life. He who comes to Me shall never hunger, and he who believes in Me shall never thirst."
John 6:35

Jesus is the True Bread, the Bread of life, because He gives us spiritual life. He nourishes our soul. Just as we need food to live physically, so also we need spiritual food to live spiritually. Without Jesus, there is no eternal life for us, but only eternal death because of our sins. Many people have plenty of meat, vegetables and fruit to eat but spiritually they are starving.

Question: Have *you* eaten of the Bread of Life?

Prayer: Dear Father in heaven, thank you for the True Bread that gives us new life.

C

is for Christ

Jesus is called the Christ,
Anointed to save the lost.
His shed blood alone sufficed
To save us and O what a cost!

"Whoever believes that Jesus is the Christ is born of God, and everyone who loves Him who begot also loves him who is begotten of Him."
1 John 5:1

The "lost" are sinners, those who have lost their way. This includes all of us, until we are saved. To sin means to break God's law. To be saved means to be delivered from the power of sin and the punishment for sin.

"Sufficed" means "was enough".

Question: Do you believe that Jesus died and rose again to save you from sin?

Prayer: Dear Father in heaven, thank You that Jesus loves us so much that He suffered and died to take away our sin.

D is for Door

Jesus alone is the Door,
Truly good news for the poor.
To save and cleanse sinners He came,
To give them new life in His name.

Jesus says, "I am the door. If anyone enters by Me, he will be saved, and will go in and out and find pasture."
John 10:9

The "poor", here, means humble, teachable people who have come to realise that they are sinners. They are truly sorry for their sins and they look to God for forgiveness. Jesus is called the Door because it is through Jesus alone that we can come to God Himself, to His presence and His loving care and provision.

Question: Do you know that Jesus is the only way to God?

Prayer: Dear Father God, thank You that in Your Son, Jesus, You provided the perfect and only way for me to become Your child.

E is for Emmanuel

Jesus, our Lord, is Emmanuel:
God has come down to be with us,
The True King and Keeper of Israel.
He, in His shelter, shall keep us.

"'Behold, the virgin shall be with child, and bear a Son, and they shall call His name Immanuel,' which is translated, 'God with us.'"
Matthew 1:23

The Name "Emmanuel" or "Immanuel" means "God is with us". God is with us through Jesus, God the Son, Who became man to reveal what God is like and to show us God's way of righteousness. Since Jesus ascended to heaven, He sent the Holy Spirit to be with us. The Holy Spirit does many things. He helps us to see that we are sinners, and brings us to repentance. He is our Helper, Comforter, and Guide. The Holy Spirit gives us understanding of God's Word, and helps us to live a holy life.

Question: Do you know that if you are God's child, He is with you always?

Prayer: Dear Father in heaven, thank You that I never need to be afraid because You are with me always.

F is for Foundation

Christ is the True Foundation,
In Zion laid, chosen and precious,
The wellspring of God's salvation,
Abounding in mercy, so gracious!

"For no other foundation can anyone lay than that which is laid, which is Jesus Christ."
1 Corinthians 3:11

"Foundation" means the base that supports a building. Just as the house we live in has a foundation which upholds it, so also our lives need a firm foundation. Our lives must be built on the only true foundation: Jesus Christ. This happens when we repent of our sins, trust in Jesus and live by His Word. (See the wonderful parable of the wise and the foolish builder, Matthew 7:24-27.)

Question: Are you building on the foundation of the solid Rock?

Prayer: Dear Father God, help me to cherish and heed Your Word always, that I may make wise choices that are pleasing to You.

G

is for God

Jesus Christ is God the Son.
Through Him were all things made;
Through His Cross, the victory won,
For there our debt was paid.

"All things were made through Him, and without Him nothing was made that was made."
John 1:3

How wonderful it is that Jesus, the Creator of the universe, walked the earth as a man 2000 years ago. How awesome it is, that He should take all our sins upon Himself and pay the penalty due to us for our sins.

Question: Do you daily praise the name of God the Son?

Prayer: Dear Father God, thank You that Jesus, through Whom all things were created, should come to earth, take human form and suffer and die so that we might live.

H is for Holy

Holy, Holy, Holy
Is the Lord, the Lord Almighty!
Be holy, says the Lord;
For He, your God, is purely holy.

"Holy, holy, holy, Lord God Almighty,
Who was and is and is to come!"
Revelation 4:8

The Bible says, again and again and again, that God is holy. It shows that God is so very pure that He is far, far above all His creation in purity and holiness. The Bible says of Jesus: "*who* is holy, harmless, undefiled, separate from sinners, and has become higher than the heavens" (Hebrews 7:26). "Separate from sinners" means that He is completely different in nature from sinners, in that He is utterly pure.

Question: Do you hallow God's name daily? To "hallow" means to keep God's name holy in your thoughts, words and deeds.

Prayer: Dear Father in heaven, help me to see how odious sin is, that I may hate all sin as you hate all sin.

I is for I AM

Jesus the Son said: "I Am."
The "I Am Who I Am" is God.
Yet humble and meek is the Lamb;
Will you follow the path He has trod?

"Jesus said to them, 'Most assuredly, I say to you, before Abraham was, I AM.'"
John 8:58

"I AM THAT I AM" is God's special name; He is self-sufficient and self-existent. When Jesus said "I AM", He showed that He is God – the second Person of the Trinity.

Question: Do you appreciate that Jesus is one with the Father since eternity?

Prayer: Dear Father God, I praise You because there is no one like You. May Your holy name be praised continually.

J is for Jesus

Jesus, the righteous, forever is Lord.
Meekly but mightily He crushed our sin.
All that are saved by His powerful blood
Are graciously changed by His Spirit within.

"But now in Christ Jesus you who once were far off have been brought near by the blood of Christ."

Ephesians 2:13

The name "Jesus" (or "Yeshua" in the original Hebrew) means Saviour. Our greatest need is to be saved from the power of sin and the punishment that sin brings.

Jesus saves us from our sin at a very high cost: His death on the Cross.

Question: Do you thank God daily for the blood of Jesus that cleanses us from all sin?

Prayer: Father in heaven, I thank You for the wonderful power of the blood of Jesus.

K is for King of Kings

Jesus Christ is King of kings:
Under His rule are all things.
Jesus Christ is Lord of lords,
Highest Sovereign, beyond all words.

"Which He will manifest in His own time, *He who is* the blessed and only Potentate, the King of kings and Lord of lords,"
1 Timothy 6:15

"Potentate" means a powerful king or ruler. Jesus Christ is the King of kings because He is the supreme ruler with all authority over all kings and all lords.

Question: Is Jesus your Lord and King?

Prayer: Dear Father God, I give You all my heart and I ask that Jesus be my Lord and King forever.

L is for Lamb of God

Our Father God promised a Lamb
Through the mouth of Abraham
No spot or blemish; the Lamb that was slain,
With Whom all His saints shall reign.

"Worthy is the Lamb who was slain
To receive power and riches and wisdom,
And strength and honour and glory and blessing!"
Revelation 5:12

Jesus is called the Lamb of God because He came from heaven to be the true and perfect sacrifice that satisfies God's holy and righteous anger against our sin.

"Sacrifice" means an offering acceptable to God. In the Old Testament a sacrifice was typically an animal that was killed and offered to God so that God would not hold the people guilty of their sin.

Question: Are you washed in the blood of the Lamb?

Prayer: Dear Father in heaven, I thank You and praise You for the blood of Jesus that washes all my sins away.

M is for Messiah

Jesus, the Messiah, was sent by the Father,
Jesus, the "Desire of the nations".
Soon all nations shall under Him gather,
Whose power knows no limitations.

"He [Andrew] first found his own brother Simon, and said to him, 'We have found the Messiah' (which is translated, the Christ)."
John 1:41

The word "Messiah" means Anointed or Chosen One. Jesus is the One anointed by God the Father as King over all the world. He willingly and lovingly laid down His life for His people to save them. Is there any greater love?

Question: Do you praise God for His amazing plan to save us?

Prayer: Dear Father God, thank You for sending the Messiah, Jesus, to deliver us from sin.

N is for Nazarene

Just as the prophets had foreseen,
Jesus was called the Nazarene.
For in Nazareth He was raised,
Whose Name shall always be praised.

"He shall be called a Nazarene."
Matthew 2:23

"Nazareth" was a town of little regard. What wonderful humility, that our Lord and Saviour Jesus should come from such a town. And indeed, Jesus Himself, "The Pearl of Great Price" (Matthew 13:45-46), was to be despised and rejected by men.

Question: Do you pray for God to keep you from all pride?

Prayer: Dear Father in heaven, help me to be humble always like Jesus, my Example and my Saviour.

O

is for Only

Begotten Son

Straight from the Father's bosom,
To show us the Father's glory,
Came Jesus the Only Begotten,
The Lion and Lamb of His-story.

"No one has seen God at any time. The only begotten Son, who is in the bosom of the Father, He has declared *Him.*"
John 1:18

"Only Begotten" means that Jesus was not created but is the eternal Son of the Father. Jesus is one with the Father, fully God as the Father is fully God. Through the *incarnation*, He became a man, fully man, while remaining fully God.

"Incarnation" refers to the act of God the Son becoming a human being.

Question: Are you thankful that Christ, your God, came and died for you?

Prayer: Dear Father God, thank you that Jesus came and showed us how holy, merciful and mighty You are.

P is for Prince of Peace

He came to set sin's captives free:
Jesus Christ, the Prince of Peace.
As the light of the gospel shines on us,
He makes our love of sin to cease.

"For unto us a Child is born,
Unto us a Son is given;
And the government will be upon His shoulder.
And His name will be called
Wonderful, Counsellor, Mighty God,
Everlasting Father, Prince of Peace."
Isaiah 9:6

Sin has brought enmity between God and man. Peaceful relationship with God is broken. But Jesus, the only Mediator between God and man, restores peace for those who repent and trust in Him.

Question: Have you made peace with God through Jesus Christ?

Prayer: Dear Father in heaven, please help many people in the world to know that only Jesus can give true peace.

Q is for Quickening Spirit

Sin, full-grown, will lead to death;
Jesus gives us life by His merit.
All that are still dead in their sin
Need Jesus, the Quickening Spirit.

"And so it is written, the first man Adam was made a living soul; the last Adam was made a quickening spirit."
1 Corinthians 15:45 (KJV)

"Quicken" is an old-fashioned word, which means to bring to life. Jesus is known as the "last Adam". By the first Adam, many were made sinners; by the second Adam, Jesus, many are made righteous (Romans 5:19).

Question: Have you spiritually been brought to life?

Prayer: Dear Father God, please quicken my friends and every member of my family that are yet to know you so that they may have eternal life.

R is for Redeemer

Our supreme Redeemer, Jesus
Gave His life so kindly for us.
Through His sinless, precious blood,
Jesus bought us back for God.

"For I know *that* my Redeemer lives,
And He shall stand at last on the earth."
Job 19:25

"Redeem" means to buy back or set free by paying a price. The best way that we can respond to such love is to show total gratitude to God. A thankful heart will accept and love God's will, and praise God in all circumstances.

Question: Do you know that you have been redeemed from sin at such a high cost?

Prayer: Dear Father in heaven, may I always thank You and praise You for the precious blood of Jesus which flowed for me at Calvary.

S is for Saviour

Chosen as Saviour of the world,
The Father sent Jesus, the Son.
Through faith in Jesus alone,
The victory over sin is won.

"For there is born to you this day in the city of David a Saviour, who is Christ the Lord."

Luke 2:11

Praise and thank God every day for the perfect love and obedience of Jesus Whose great sacrifice brought us back to God.

Question: Is there any other Saviour besides Jesus? Have you trusted in Jesus to save you?

Prayer: Dear Father God, please help those who doubt to know that there is no Saviour besides Jesus.

B
C

T is for Teacher

Jesus, the Master Teacher,
Said every word with power,
Our perfect Example and Preacher,
Unmatched in His use of each hour.

"This man came to Jesus by night and said to Him, 'Rabbi, we know that You are a teacher come from God; for no one can do these signs that You do unless God is with him.'"
John 3:2

Jesus was called "Rabbi", which means "Teacher", by the crowds of people that followed Him.

The people were amazed by the authority and power of His teaching. His disciples also addressed Him by the title "Teacher".

Question: Do you daily spend time in the Bible, listening to the Master Teacher? Do you believe and live by every word that comes from His mouth? (Deuteronomy 8:3)

Prayer: Dear Father in heaven, thank You for Your Word. I pray that You give me a deep love of Your precious Word and the power to obey You always.

U is for Unspeakable Gift

What love, mercy and grace,
Divine and far beyond words,
That Christ, the Unspeakable Gift,
Should die for the lost and adrift.

"Thanks be to God for His unspeakable gift!"
2 Corinthians 9:15 (ASV)

"Unspeakable gift" means that the gift is so precious that words cannot express its value.

What words can adequately describe the infinite worth of the gift of Jesus to unworthy sinners?

Question: Have you given thanks today for the wonderful gift of Jesus?

Prayer: Dear Father in heaven, please help me to tell my friends about Jesus that they may know the Power of God that saves from sin.

V is for Vine

Jesus, our Lord, is the True Vine;
True followers of Christ are the branches.
In Christ abide: you will steadfastly shine
With a godliness nothing else matches.

"I am the vine, you *are* the branches. He who abides in Me, and I in him, bears much fruit; for without Me you can do nothing."
John 15:5

Jesus describes Himself as the Vine because His true followers, the branches, are one with Him. The branches are joined to Him and totally depend on Him. We bear spiritual fruit as we are enabled and sustained by Him.

Question: Are you staying so very near to Jesus today?

Prayer: Dear Father God, please keep me close to You, and make me more and more like Jesus, my Saviour.

W is for WORD

Jesus Christ is the Word,
The glorious expression of God.
Hear Him, love Him, obey Him,
And so show that He is Your Lord.

"In the beginning was the Word,
And the Word was with God,
And the Word was God."
John 1:1

Jesus, the Word, is the expression of God. He shows us the nature of God and gives us the message of God. He is the Truth and He bears witness to the Truth.

The Bible says that Jesus, the Word of God, is coming back! He comes on a white horse and out of His mouth goes a sharp two-edged sword that will smite the nations that remain in rebellion against God (Rev. 19:13-15).

Question: Do you love to hear and obey the Word?

Prayer: Dear Father in heaven, may Your precious Word fill my heart and may Your Spirit give me the power to live righteously.

X is for eXcellent and eXalted

Jesus, far mightier than angels,
Jesus, more excellent is His name!
Children, even babies, show forth His praise,
Confounding and shaming His foes.

"When He had by Himself purged our sins, sat down at the right hand of the Majesty on high, having become so much better than the angels, as He has by inheritance obtained a more excellent name than they."
Hebrews 1:3-4

Jesus, the excellent One, accomplished the holy will of the Father through His perfect obedience. Therefore, God exalted Him to the highest place. The Bible says that every knee shall bow and every tongue confess that Jesus Christ is Lord to the glory of God the Father (Phil. 2:10-11).

Question: Do you praise and daily exalt the name of Jesus?

Prayer: Dear Father God, fill me with love and adoration of Jesus. May I continually confess that "Jesus is Lord".

Y is for YHWH ["Yahweh"]

God said: "I am YHWH thy God".
What a sacred and special Name
For our glorious Creator and Lord,
The great "I Am who I Am".

"Oh, magnify the LORD with me,
And let us exalt His name together."
Psalm 34:3

YHWH (Yahweh) is the Hebrew personal Name of God revealed by God. It shows us that God is active, self-existing, self-sufficient and all-powerful.

Question: Have you submitted to Yahweh? Do you daily sing His praise?

Prayer: Dear Father in heaven, may I forever be in awe of You.

Z is for Zion

Out of Zion, city of glory
Shines perfection: God's very presence!
Beautiful Zion, pure and holy,
City of joy, His saints' inheritance!

"Out of Zion, the perfection of beauty,
God will shine forth."
Psalm 50:2

Zion refers to Jerusalem, the city of David.

Spiritually, Zion refers to the city of God, the heavenly Jerusalem, where His saints will one day dwell forever.

We become citizens of beautiful Zion through our new birth in Christ – Hallelujah!

Question: Do you long to live in Zion, the eternal city of God?

Prayer: Dear Father in heaven, I pray that You may say of me:

"This one was born there." [Zion]
Psalm 87:6

Doxology

Scripture commands us to give thanks in everything for this is the will of God. (1 Thessalonians 5:18). You may end your devotion time with a thanksgiving doxology (praise) such as:

Revelation 5:12, "Worthy is the Lamb that was slain to receive power, and riches, and wisdom, and strength, and honour, and glory, and blessing!"

Revelation 1:5b-6, "To Him who loved us and washed us from our sins in His own blood, and has made us kings and priests to His God and Father, to Him be glory and dominion forever and ever. Amen."

1 Timothy 1:17, "Now to the King eternal, immortal, invisible, to God who alone is wise, *be* honour and glory forever and ever. Amen."

Revelation 7:12, "Amen! Blessing and glory and wisdom, thanksgiving and honour and power and might, *be* to our God forever and ever. Amen."

Maranatha: Come, Lord Jesus!

A Child's Prayer of Salvation

It is good indeed to study and to know the wonderful names of Jesus; but remember that this knowledge will not, in and of itself, meet your greatest need, which is to be saved and reconciled to God. With the Fall, when our first parents, Adam and Eve, disobeyed God's command, sin entered the world. God's beautiful world was horribly marred. Everyone born after this terrible rebellion is born with an inescapably sinful nature. Our hearts are totally corrupted by sin. Our tendency is always towards sinning, we love to sin. Sin, as we have seen, leads to eternal death and separation from God. But God, in His great love and mercy, made a way for our sins to be forgiven and washed away by the sacrifice of Jesus Christ at the Cross.

As we have seen, God is totally holy. All those who wish to become children of God must have their sins forgiven by God. They must completely turn away from sin and put all their trust in Jesus, our only Saviour, Who paid our sin debt on the Cross at Calvary. When this happens to an individual, it becomes just as if he or she had never sinned! Here is a sample prayer for salvation that may be used.

Dear Father God,

I believe and I thank You that Jesus died for me and rose again, so that I could be forgiven, and He is now in heaven with You. Thank you for helping me, through Your Word, to see how horrible sin is. I ask You to forgive me my sin, wash me clean, and come into my heart and give me a new life. Help me, from now on, always to know that Jesus is Lord over my life. Give me the Holy Spirit, so that I can have the power through Him to live for You as Your child, knowing that one day I will be with You, my God and my Saviour, forever.

In Jesus' Name,

Amen

Hymn (Thou Whose Name is Called Jesus)

Ponder and sing the words of this beautiful hymn by Jean Sophia Piggott (1845–1882):

Thou whose name is called Jesus,
Risen Lord of life and pow'r,
Oh, it is so sweet to trust Thee,
Every day and every hour;
Of Thy wondrous grace I sing,
Saviour, Counsellor, and King.

Thou canst keep my feet from falling,
Even my poor wayward feet;
Thou who dost present me faultless
In Thee—Righteousness complete;
Jesus, Lord, in knowing Thee,
Oh, what strength and victory.

All the sin in me, my Saviour,
Thou canst conquer and subdue;
With Thy sanctifying power
Permeate my spirit through;
Let Thy government increase,
Risen, crowned, Prince of Peace.

Thou canst keep me upward looking,
Ever upward in Thy face;
Thou canst make me stand, upholden
By the greatness of Thy grace;
Every promise of Thy word
Now I claim from Thee, dear Lord.

Oh! What joy to trust Thee, Jesus,
Mighty Victor o'er the grave,
And to learn amid earth's shadows
Thine unceasing power to save!
Only those who prove Thee know
What the grace Thou dost bestow.

Make my life a bright outshining
Of Thy life, that all may see
Thine own resurrection power
Mightily put forth in me;
Ever let my heart become
Yet more consciously Thy home.

Here are some other magnificent names and titles of our Lord Jesus:

A

Almighty	Revelation 1:8
Author of Eternal Salvation	Hebrews 5:9
Amen	Revelation 3:14
Advocate	1 John 2:1
Altogether Lovely	Song of Solomon 5:16

B

Beloved	Matthew 12:18
Bright and Morning Star	Revelation 22:16
Branch	Isaiah 4:2
Bread of God	John 6:33

C

Creator	John 1:3
Cornerstone	Psalm 118:22
Captain of Salvation	Hebrews 2:10
Chosen by God	1 Peter 2:4

D

Dayspring	Luke 1:78
Deliverer	Romans 11:26
Desire of All Nations	Haggai 2:7

E

Eternal Life	1 John 1:2
Elect One	Isaiah 42:1
Everlasting Father	Isaiah 9:6

F

Faithful	1 Thessalonians 5:24
Fountain	Zechariah 13:1
Friend	Proverbs 18:24
Firstborn from the Dead	Revelation 1:5

G

Gift of God	John 4:10
Glory of the Lord	Isaiah 40:5
Guide	Psalm 48:14
Great High Priest	Hebrews 4:14

H

Holy One	Psalm 16:10
Head	Colossians 1:18
Heir of All Things	Hebrews 1:2
Hope of Israel	Acts 28:20

I

Immortal	1 Timothy 1:17
Image of the Invisible God	Colossians 1:15

J

Just One	Acts 7:52
Judge of All the Earth	Genesis 18:25

K

King of Glory	Psalm 24:7-8
King of the Saints	Revelation 15:3
King of Israel	John1:49

L

Light of the World	John 8:12
Life	John 14:6
Lion of the Tribe of Judah	Revelation 5:5
Last Adam	1 Corinthians 15:45
Lord of Glory	1 Corinthians 2:8

M

Mediator	1 Timothy 2:5
Mighty God	Isaiah 9:6
Morning Star	Revelation 22:16

N

Name Which is Above Every Name	Philippians 2:9

O

Only Wise God	1 Timothy 1:17
Only Potentate	1 Timothy 6:15
Offering and a Sacrifice	Ephesians 5:2
Our Great God and Saviour	Titus 2:13
Our Redemption	1 Corinthians 1:30

P

Physician	Matthew 9:12
Potentate	1 Timothy 6:15
Power of God	1 Corinthians 1:24
Prince of Life	Acts 3:15
Prophet	John 7:40

R

Rabbi	John 3:2
Rock	1 Corinthians 10:4

Refiner's Fire	Malachi 3:2
Refuge	Isaiah 25:4
Righteous Branch	Jeremiah 23:5
Ruler of God's Creation	Revelation 3:14

S

Servant	Matthew 12:18
Shepherd	Mark 14:27
Sun of Righteousness	Malachi 4:2
Shiloh	Genesis 49:10
Son of Man	Matthew 8:20
Son of God	John 1:49
Son of the Highest	Luke 1:32

T

True Witness	Revelation 3:14
True Vine	John 15:1
True Light	John 1:9
The One Mediator	1Timothy 2:5
The Stone the Builders Rejected	Acts 4:11

U

Undefiled	Hebrews 7:26

V

Very Christ	Acts 9:22

W

Way	John 14:6
Word of God	Revelation 19:13
Wonderful	Isaiah 9:6
Wisdom of God	1 Corinthians 1:24
Worthy	Revelation 5:9

JESUS
The Word
Rock
Messiah
Morning Star
Saviour
Emmanuel
Name above all names
Alpha and Omega
True Vine
Wonderful
Light of the World
Shiloh
The Good Shepherd
Lamb of God
King of Glory
Mediator